2013

2015

2007

2008

„Das Überstreichen, eigentlich das Schwärzen der Wände ist für mich auch eine Wiedergeburt, eine Rückkehr von den (schon bald Un-)Toten: ein Weckruf für die Stadt und ihre Bewohner, eine Mahnung zur Notwendigkeit der Erhaltung von bezahlbaren und lebenswerten Räumen, anstatt untote Kunstpräparate zu produzieren. Es fordert einen Dialog mit der Realität der Stadt an, betont das Potential und die gesellschaftliche Funktion künstlerischer Interventionen dort, wo andere Mittel an ihre Grenzen stoßen."

„For me the white – well, in this case – black-washing also signifies a rebirth, a return from the (soon to be un)dead: As a wake-up call to the city and its dwellers, a reminder of the necessity to preserve the affordable and lively spaces of possibility, instead of producing undead taxidermies of art. It promts a dialoge with the city's reality stressing the capability and social function of artistic interventions where others fail to advance."

Lutz Henke, Artitude Kunstverein (Zitat aus: The Guardian, 19.12.2014)

LITTLE LUCY
balu
WORLD
SALMAN SAYS
KUNST
MICH
MAL...
RIOT
BITTE STIRB
SWORD

Kai Jakob

Street Art in Berlin

Jaron Verlag

Reclaim the Streets

Inhalt

Contents

FUCK
STRE
ART

Vorwort

„Street Art in Berlin" liegt nun in seiner siebenten Ausgabe vor. Das Interesse an der urbanen Kunstform scheint ungebrochen, und das freut mich sehr. Dieses Buch reflektierte immer das aktuelle Geschehen auf der Straße. Street Art ist in einem steten Prozess der Veränderung, und deshalb muss sich auch ein Buch, das sich der Street Art widmet, unentwegt zu verändern versuchen. Nur so kann es als eine Art zweidimensionale Galerie die Gegenwart abbilden, ohne zu einem verstaubten Museum zu werden.

Aus gegebenem Anlass besinnt sich diese Ausgabe in ihrem Cover auf die Anfänge. Das Wandbild von Blu in all seinen Veränderungen über die Jahre hinweg begleitete dieses Buch von Anfang an. Ende 2014 wurde es vom Künstler und lokalen Aktivisten selbst übermalt – ein politisches Statement. Dieses Buch zeichnet die Veränderungen nach und visualisiert den Prozess der Transformation des Kunstwerks bis in die Gegenwart.

Außerdem sind auch in dieser Ausgabe wieder viele neue Bilder hinzugekommen, ältere wurden ersetzt. Street Art ist in Berlin nach wie vor sehr vital. Ich möchte einen Überblick verschaffen und dem Leser ein Gefühl dafür vermitteln, was Street Art ist und wie sie sich in Berlin verkörpert. Ich hoffe, dass mir das auch mit dieser Ausgabe wieder gelingt, und wünsche viel Freude an dem Buch.

Malt die Städte ... **schwarz**!?

Foreword

This is the 7th printing of "Street Art in Berlin." I am very happy that interest in this urban art form continues to be strong. This book is also a reflection of what is happening on the streets right now. Street Art is always in a process of change, so a book dedicated to Street Art has to try to keep up. That is the only way it can illustrate the now as a two-dimensional gallery without becoming a dusty museum.

In light of recent events, the cover of this edition has returned to its beginnings. The mural by Blu with all the changes it underwent over the years has accompanied this book from the start. At the end of 2014, the artist and local activists painted it over – a political statement. This book documents the changes and shows how this work of art has transformed into its current form.

In this edition many new pictures have been added that replace older ones. Street Art continues to be important in Berlin. I want to present an overview and convey to readers what Street Art is and how it manifests itself in Berlin. I hope I have achieved that with this edition too and that you have fun with this book.

*Paint the cities ... **black**!?*

El Bocho

Definition Street Art

Street Art (auch als Street-Art oder Streetart, seltener eingedeutscht als Straßenkunst bezeichnet) ist dem Begriff der Urban Art unterstellt und beschreibt allgemein eine für jeden zugängliche künstlerische Ausdrucksform im öffentlichen Raum. Dazu zählen Graffiti in den verschiedensten Formen genauso wie **Stickerart** (Kunst mit Aufklebern), **Stencils** (auch **Pochoirs**, Schablonengraffiti), **Collagen** und **Decollagen**, **Scratchiti** (Einkratzen in harte Oberflächen), **Cut-outs** (Herausschneiden des eigentlichen Werks), **Direkter Farbauftrag**, **Roll-ons** (großflächiger Schriftzug mittels Farbwalzen), **Tape Art** (Aufbringen von Klebestreifen), **Chipping** (das Fragmentieren von Oberflächen), **Tile Board** (auf stabilem Trägermaterial aufgebrachtes Kunstwerk), **Kreidezeichnung**, **Ad-Busting** (das Verändern von Werbeplakaten), **Urban Knitting** (das Einfassen von Gegenständen mit Strickware), elektronische Umsetzungen mittels **LED-Technik** oder **Videoprojektion**, **Folierung** (das Anbringen und/oder Einwickeln von Gegenständen im Straßenraum mit Frischhaltefolie) sowie Installationen oder Umbauten in einer vom Künstler ausgewählten Umgebung.

Die Künstler bleiben oft anonym oder sind nur einem kleinen Kreis von Personen bekannt. Unter den Akteuren gibt es den Ausruf „Reclaim the Streets" – die Straßen zurückerobern. Er bezieht sich auf eine Kritik an der flächendeckenden Werbung in den Städten, an einem einheitlich geordneten Erscheinungsbild und der Unisexifizierung der Stadträume. Street Art geht meist mit einem Gesetzesbruch einher (zum Beispiel Sachbeschädigung bzw. „Verunstaltung" und Wildplakatierung). Die Künstler selbst sehen jedoch keine illegale Handlung in ihrem Tun.

Street-Art-Künstler „werben" in ihren Werken für sich selbst und für eine Einstellung oder einen Gedanken. Damit werben sie für ein Individuum und nicht für ein Produkt im klassischen Sinne. Häufig finden sich Arbeiten, welche die Werbung oder gesellschaftliche Zustände parodieren. Ihr Handeln wird von den Künstlern oft mit dem Bedürfnis begründet, das öffentliche Straßenbild individuell mitzugestalten, einen Gegenpol zur dominanten Wirkung der kommerziellen Werbung und Oberflächlichkeit zu bilden und sich selbst kreativ zu verwirklichen. Aktuell ist in der Szene zu beobachten, dass sich Street Art teilweise aus dem „Untergrund" herausbewegt, auf dem Kunstmarkt Einzug hält und von der Mainstream-Kultur vereinnahmt wird. Ebenso findet Street Art auch vermehrt im Internet statt und bekommt so einen virtuellen Spielort. Somit entwickelt sich die Street Art weiter, und es bleibt abzuwarten, wie sich deren Begrifflichkeit in der Zukunft definieren lassen wird.

Definition of Street Art

*Street art (a subgroup of **Urban Art**) refers to a form of artistic expression found in public spaces and thus openly accessible to everyone. It includes many different forms of graffiti as well as **sticker art** and **stencils** (also known as **pochoirs**), **collage** and **decollage**, **scratchiti** (etching into hard surfaces), **cut-outs** (literally the cutting out of the actual work of art), **direct application of paint**, **roll-ons** (large scaled characters via inking rollers) **tape-art** (pasting adhesive tape strips), **chipping** (the chipping of a surface), **tile-board** (artwork on solid carrier material), **crayon**, **ad-busting** (the alteration of advertisement posters), **urban knitting** (wrapping objects in yarn), electronic light presentations using **LED technology** or **video projection**, **plastic wrapping** (fastening or wrapping objects on the street using cling wrap) and installations and rebuilding at a place selected by the artist.*

Street artists almost always remain anonymous or are known only to a small circle of people. "Reclaim the Streets" is a popular slogan among graffiti artists, referring to their critical view of pervasive advertising in cities, uniform appearances and the unisexualization of urban space. Street art usually entails illicit action (for example damage to property, defacement and unauthorized placards). The artists, however, do not see anything unlawful in what they are doing.

Street artists promote themselves, their attitudes or specific ideas in their work. Thus they are "advertising" for an individual and not a product in the classical sense. Their works are often a parody of an existing advertisement. Artists explain their motivation as stemming from a need to personally design public space, to provide an alternative to the dominant impact of commercial advertising and its superficiality, and as an outlet to express their creativity. What becomes clear in observing the current street-art scene is that it is emerging from the "underground," finding its way into the art market and into the mainstream. Street Art is also taking place increasingly on the Internet, which provides a virtual playground. Thus Street Art continues to progress and it remains open how its concepts will develop in the future.

Herkunft und Entwicklung der Street Art

Im klassischen Sinne war die Straßenkunst früher gesellschaftlich akzeptiert. Man verstand unter Straßenkunst beispielsweise einen Pantomimen, diverse Künstler mit ihren Darbietungen oder auch Maler, die als öffentliche Attraktionen agierten – also Kunst im öffentlichen Raum. Darum geht es bei Street Art im eigentlichen Sinne auch.

Bereits der italienische Maler Giotto benutzte bei seinen Fresken Schablonen. Später arbeiteten auch Künstler wie Kandinsky, Klee, Matisse und Andy Warhol mit dieser Technik, die einen großen Anteil an der heutigen Street Art ausmacht.

Ausgangspunkt der Street Art ist die Graffiti-Szene. Das Wort „Graffito" ist vulgärlateinisch und bedeutet etwa „mit dem Griffel kratzen". Als urbane Sprache des Ghettos entstand eine neue Stilform, die sich schnell verbreitete. Hierbei vermutet man in **Cornbread** und **Taki 183** zwei der frühen Mitbegründer der Graffiti-Welle. Graffiti gehören heute zu den festen Bestandteilen der Hip-Hop-Bewegung. Im Laufe der Zeit entwickelten sich viele Interpretationsformen, weg von den Schriftzügen hin zu dem, was wir heute allgemein unter Street Art verstehen. Zwar kann man nach wie vor Street Art zur Ausdrucksform des Graffito zählen, dennoch hat sich im Laufe der Zeit die Graffiti-Kunst als abgegrenzte Einzeldisziplin entwickelt und steht für eine andere Intention.

Eine Form von Street Art sind **Pochoirs**, auch **Stencils** genannt. In Europa begann in Paris Anfang der 1980er Jahre unter anderem **Blek le Rat**, mit Schablonenkunst auf verschiedenen Untergründen der Stadt zu arbeiten und diese zu verbreiten. Das war die Geburtsstunde der flächenmäßigen Verbreitung von **Pochoirs** in Europa, wenn man von den zuvor genannten Künstlern und den Höhlenmalereien der Urzeit absieht, in der unsere Vorfahren bereits mit der Negativtechnik arbeiteten, als sie Gegenstände mit Farbe umzeichneten und an den Wänden hinterließen.

Eine Abgrenzung von Graffiti zu Street Art ist wie folgt zu erklären: Während der allgemeine Tenor Graffiti als Verschandelung des Stadtbildes verurteilt, sehen die Menschen in Street Art oftmals keinen störenden Eingriff in das städtische Erscheinungsbild, obwohl im Grundsatz kaum ein Unterschied zwischen beiden Ausdrucksformen vorhanden zu sein scheint. Diese allgemein höhere Akzeptanz liegt sicherlich darin begründet, dass Street Art versucht, sich zu integrieren, anstatt aggressiv zu provozieren; auch die leichtere Lesbarkeit ist ihr vermutlich zuträglich. Es herrschen mehr Feinsinn, Humor und Intellekt. Die Künstler wollen das Stadtbild in ihrem Sinne verschönern, prägen und beleben. Der öffentliche Raum soll nach eigenem Ermessen umgestaltet werden – weg von Stereotypie, Langeweile, Ersetzbarkeit, Kontrolle und Monotonie, die oftmals in den Städten herrschen. In erster Linie geht es um eine Infragestellung der oft hingenommenen Einschränkungen des öffentlichen Raumes. Es herrscht eine Omnipräsenz der Werbung, die sich stark des urbanen Raumes bedient und sich diesen regelrecht einverleibt. Hinzu kommen Einschränkungen und Verbote,

Origins and Evolution of Street Art

In the past traditional street art was socially accepted. It included pantomime, various artistic performances and artists whose painting became a public attraction. It was art created in public space. This is what street art today is still about.

The 14th century Italian artist Giotto had already applied the use of stencils in his frescos. Later, other artists such as Kandinsky, Klee, Matisse and Andy Warhol, applied many of the same techniques that are used by street artists today.

Modern street art began with graffiti. The word "graffito" is crude Latin meaning "to scratch with the pen." A new manner of expression emerged and quickly spread within the urban ghetto. It is presumed that ***Cornbread*** *and* ***Taki 183*** *were two of the early cofounders of the graffiti scene. Today graffiti is a definitive part of the hip-hop movement. Over time a number of different interpretive forms developed which moved away from writing and toward what we generally understand today by the term "street art." Street art can still count as a form of graffiti, but over time graffiti became more narrowly defined as a distinct discipline with a different intention.*

Pochoirs*, also known as* ***stencils****, is one form of street art. In Europe, in the early 1980s,* ***Blek le Rat****, in Paris, was one of the first to work with stencil art, spreading it on various surfaces throughout the city. That was the beginning of widespread* ***pochoirs*** *in Europe, if we don't count the artists mentioned above or the caveman paintings of primitive times in which our ancestors experimented with the negative technique of tracing objects on the wall with color.*

The difference between graffiti and street art can be explained as follows: The general public tends to criticize graffiti as vandalism, a defacement of the city's appearance. Street art, however, offers less offense, although in principle there isn't much difference in these two forms of expression. There is a higher degree of tolerance for street art because it's usually more integrated into its surroundings than graffiti which serves to provoke. Street art is easier to read which also makes it more acceptable. It encompasses more subtlety, humor and intellect. The artists aim to beautify, imprint and revive the city according to their own tastes. They want to redesign public space as they see fit, moving away from stereotypes, exchangeability, control and monotony that is so prevalent in cities. Foremost, however, the artists use street art to question the limitations placed on public space, limitations that are generally tolerated by the public. Like, for example, the fact that advertising overwhelming intrudes on public spaces everywhere for its own benefit and at the expense of urban space. Or the many signs on the streets announcing restrictions and bans, suggesting that public space is not really there for its residents to use freely after all. In truth the urban space is organized through and through to serve a specific function, but it is not intended

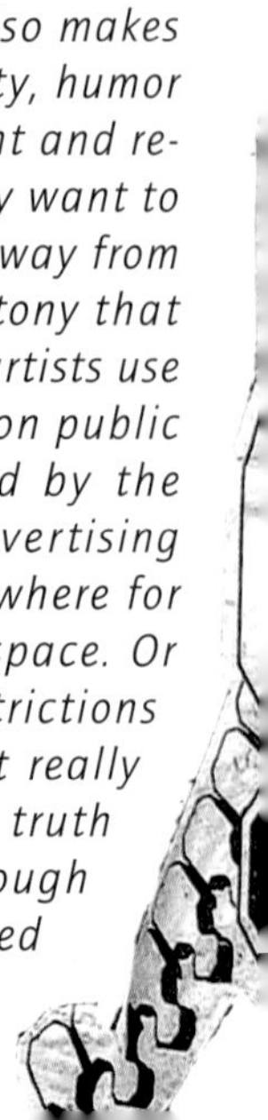

die in Form von Schildern auftreten. Also handelt es sich nur scheinbar um einen tatsächlich offenen Raum für die Bewohner. In der Realität ist der urbane Raum durchorganisiert und funktionalistisch, keinesfalls ein Kommunikationsraum der Bürger. Es geht also auch um eine Zurückeroberung.

Street Art ist eine subkulturelle, kreative Ausdrucksform im Kontext der Straße, eine Art der menschlichen Kommunikation. Es ist eine kreative Art der Entfaltung, eine Mitgestaltung und Selbstdarstellung als Reaktion auf die Realität. Die Erschaffung von Neuem und Fiktionalem, das Darstellen von Zuständen. Der öffentliche Raum ist die Benutzerschnittstelle der Stadt, ein Ort der Kommunikation. Street Art ist also auch ein Indikator für ungebundenes kreatives Potential an Orten, welche die Menschen interessieren. In der städtischen Semiotik ist Street Art ein offenes und in Veränderung stehendes Kommunikationssystem. Street Art kann ohne den städtischen Kontext nicht bestehen und ist vergänglich. Was heute noch da ist, kann morgen schon wieder weg sein. Das ist die Voraussetzung für eine stetige Weiterentwicklung und Erneuerung. Man kann ständig Neues erschaffen und viele, oft unerwartete und unvorhergesehene Entdeckungen machen. Die Stadt wird zur Galerie. Dabei bedienen sich die Künstler vielseitiger visueller Ausdrucksformen durch Zeichen, Kodierungen, Elemente und Symbole. Ob gemalt, aufgeklebt, gesprüht oder installiert, es gibt vielerlei Möglichkeiten, seine Botschaften sichtbar zu verbreiten. Mit Aufklebern, Tapete, Kleister, Poster, Collagen, Fotokopien, dreidimensionalen Gebilden, Kreide, Folien und Schablonen werden bewusst ausgesuchte Fassaden, Trafo-Häuschen, Bauwagen, Zäune, Werbewände, Bahnen und Straßen mit Parolen, Bildern, Nachrichten und Logos verziert. Street Art ist eine Zeichenkultur. Hierbei ist der Kontext des Ortes und seines Untergrundes genauso wichtig wie die Kunst an sich. Die Orte, die Straßen und die Fassaden werden lesbar. Hat man sich daran gewöhnt und es angenommen, so erscheinen alle anderen zuvor angeführten sterilen und monotonen Orte wie Bücher mit unbeschriebenen Seiten – leer und inhaltslos, verlassen und langweilig.

Street Art kann als kreativer Fehler des Systems begriffen werden. Ein Fehler, der sich so stark einbringen konnte, dass er bereits adaptiert wird und von dem, was er kritisiert und in Frage stellt, benutzt wird: Werbung und Medien bedienen sich des kreativen Potentials und machen es zu ihrem; eine scheinbar feindliche Übernahme. Daraus folgt, dass Street Art nun verstärkt im gesellschaftlichen Kontext wahrgenommen wird. Auch wenn „Schablonendenken" allgemein eher vermieden werden sollte, ist es in der Street Art mehr als gewollt. Es ist eine sehr kreative Analyse der Realität, ein Spiegel der Gesellschaft. Interessant ist dabei, ob und wie sich Street Art weiterentwickeln kann und wird. Moderne Techniken, beispielsweise LED und Laserprojektionen, zeigen den Weg dazu auf.

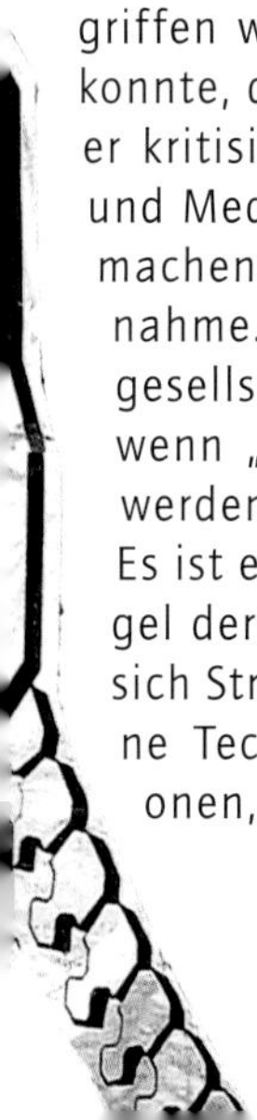

as a space for communication between citizens. In this sense, street art is about re-conquering public spaces.

It is a subcultural, creative form of expression which is articulated in the streets. It is a form of human communication. It is a creative form of development, which involves active participation and self-presentation as a reaction to reality. It is the creation of something new and fictional and a depiction of the state of things. Public space is the user gateway to the city, a place of communication. Street art is thus also an indicator of the unbound, creative potential at places that interest people. In urban semiotics, street art is an open and ever-changing system of communication. It cannot exist without the urban context and it remains transient. What is here today may be gone tomorrow. That is the prerequisite for its constant growth and renewal. The artists are consistently able to create something new and to make many unexpected and unpredictable discoveries. The city becomes a gallery. The artists engage in eclectic visual forms of expression using drawing, coding, elements and symbols. Messages can be spread and made visible through any number of methods, be it pasted, sprayed or installed. The artists use stickers, wall paper, glue, posters, collages, photocopies, three-dimensional images, chalk, foil and stencils to cover carefully selected façades such as transformer boxes, construction trailers, fences, advertising panels, trams and streets with slogans, pictures, news, and logos. Street art is a drawing culture in which the context of the site and its surface is equally as important as the art itself. The location, the street and the façade, become readable. Once the public has become accustomed to the art and learned to accept it, sites that were previously sterile and monotone seem like a book with bare pages – empty and without content, deserted and dull.

Street art can also be understood as a creative error in the system. An error that was able to position itself so firmly that it is adapted and used by that very thing which it aims to criticize and question: Advertising and media have taken advantage of the creative potential of street art and adopted it as their own – an apparently hostile takeover. This, in turn, has led street art to be more strongly recognized within society. Although stereotyped thinking, in general, is to be avoided, it is more than desirable in street art. It is a very creative process permeating reality, and changing our reflection of society. It will be interesting to see whether and how street art continues to develop. Modern techniques, LED and laser projection, for example, give an indication of where it is heading in the future.

STREET ART

THE BERLIN
URBAN ART
COLLECTIVE

Street Art in Berlin

Dieses Buch stellt Street Art in und aus Berlin vor. In kaum einer anderen Stadt trifft man momentan eine so große und vielfältige Verbreitung von Street Art an wie an den Mauern und in den Straßen Berlins. Das Dasein als ehemals geteilte Frontstadt des Kalten Krieges, als Stadt der zwei entgegengesetzten politischen Systeme, als alte und neue Hauptstadt, als Transitstadt im Herzen Europas, Kulturstadt und – wie von der UNESCO betitelt – als „Stadt des Designs" verleiht Berlin seinen ganz speziellen Status mit seiner ganz eigenen Ausstrahlung und einem besonderen Charme.

Nach dem Fall der Mauer waren einige Teile im Osten der Stadt verlassen; es herrschte Leerstand. Nach und nach zog es Künstler, Musiker und viele andere Menschen in diese leerstehenden Gegenden. Es begann eine Zeit des Aufbruchs. Nachdem Berlin wieder Hauptstadt geworden war, entwickelte sich ein regelrechter Boom der Stadt.

Die Mieten sind gerade im Ostteil weiterhin günstig, es gibt mehr Platz als Nachfrage, und somit ist und bleibt die Stadt gerade für Künstler und kreativ arbeitende Menschen attraktiv. Der finanzielle Druck bleibt überschaubar, und man findet den benötigten Freiraum. Aus der ganzen Welt sammeln sich junge Menschen in der Stadt und bilden zusammen eine große und stetig wachsende kreative Szene. Im Laufe der Zeit sind Galerien, unabhängige Ladengeschäfte, kleine Verlage, Agenturen und Ausstellungen regelrecht aus dem Boden geschossen.

In unzähligen universitären, schulischen und freien Bildungseinrichtungen, die die unterschiedlichsten kreativen Ausbildungen anbieten, kann man seine Kreativität festigen und ausbauen. Designer, Bildhauer, Maler, Grafiker, Fotografen, Galeristen, freie Künstler und Modeschaffende finden in Berlin eine gute Infrastruktur für ihre Arbeiten – gemischt aus Inspiration, Freiraum, Forum und Nachfrage. Man findet alles zwischen Spontan-Aktion, freien No-Budget-Projekten, kommerziellen Arbeiten und Mainstream. Jeder kann seinen Platz finden. Berlin ist Ort der stetigen Veränderung, aber zugleich auch ein dauerhaft unfertiger Ort. Gerade in Vierteln wie Friedrichshain, Kreuzberg, Mitte und Prenzlauer Berg kann man dies beobachten, dort zentriert sich das kreative Leben in all seinen Facetten. Diese Viertel sind starke Identifikationsorte ihrer Bewohner, also auch Kommunikationsräume. Kommunikation findet hier auf unterschiedlichste Art und Weise statt, und Street Art ist eine sehr ausgeprägte Form davon. Als Indikator für ein ungebundenes kreatives Potential der Orte, an welchen man Street Art findet, kann diese aufzeigen, wie stark die in den Vierteln lebenden Menschen ihren öffentlichen Freiraum mitgestalten und bewusst beeinflussen wollen. Weg vom allgemein geltenden Kodex, weg von Steuerung und Monotonie, hin zu Kritik, Infragestellung, Umgestaltung und Eigendefinition. Und das in einer kreativen Vielfalt, die gleichermaßen interessiert und begeistert. Die Oberflächen der Stadt werden zu einer großen Galerie.

Street Art in Berlin

This book presents street art in and from Berlin. Berlin is currently one of the few cities with such a large and eclectic collection of street art on its walls and streets. Berlin is the formerly divided frontline city of the Cold War, once a city with two opposing political systems, an old and a new capital, a transit city in the heart of Europe, a cultural city, designated by UNESCO as the "City of Design." All this lends Berlin a special status, and adds to its unique charisma and charm.

After the Wall fell some areas in the eastern half of the city were deserted. A sense of vacancy prevailed. Little by little artists, musicians and lots of other people began to settle in these empty areas. A new era began. After Berlin re-established itself as the national capital, the city began to boom.

Rents in the eastern parts of the city are still low. The space available is greater than the demand, making the city attractive to artists and other creative people. The city remains affordable and there is enough space for everyone. Young people from all over the world meet in Berlin and together form a large and continually growing creative scene. Over time, galleries, independent shops, small publishers, agencies and exhibitions have literally sprung up out of nowhere.

Any number of universities, schools and independent educational institutions offer training to people interested in developing and improving their creative skills. Designers, sculptors, painters, graphic artists, photographers, gallery owners, independent artists and fashion designers find a good infrastructure for their work in Berlin – a mix of inspiration, space, forum and demand. You can find everything here ranging from spontaneous activities and free no-budget projects to commercial works in the mainstream. There is something for everyone. Berlin is a place that is forever changing, but which also remains permanently unfinished. This is especially true in neighborhoods like Friedrichshain, Kreuzberg, Mitte and Prenzlauer Berg where a multi-faceted creative life has established itself. The residents of these districts identify strongly with their neighborhoods. Communication takes place in them in many different ways and street art is one of its more distinct forms. Street Art is an indication of the free creative potential of a neighborhood and shows how strongly the residents wish to participate and consciously influence the design of public space. It is a move away from the generally accepted codex, from control and monotony, and a step towards criticism, questioning, redesign and personal definition. And it does this with such a degree of diversity that it both interests and inspires. The surfaces of the city emerge as a large gallery.

Stencils

Stencil steht für ein Graffito mit Schablonen, daher auch die Bezeichnung Schablonengraffito. Es funktioniert als eine Art Freiluft-Siebdruck und entstand in den 1970er Jahren in Frankreich (auch **Pochoir** genannt). Seine erste Blütezeit hatte es in den 1980er Jahren in Paris. Im Englischen wird dieser Stil **stencil art** genannt.

Im Gegensatz zum Graffito benötigt das **Stencil** einiges an Vorbereitung für die Anfertigung von Schablonen. Diese werden in der Regel aus Pappe, aber auch aus Kunststoff oder laminiertem Papier, seltener aus Holz oder Metall gefertigt und eignen sich für die häufige Wiederholung eines Motivs im Straßenbild. Komplizierte und großflächige Artefakte werden auf allen möglichen Untergründen montiert. Durch die Kombination verschiedener Schablonen und Farben entsteht so eine schier unendliche Vielfalt an Möglichkeiten. **Stencils** werden oftmals auch zur Verbreitung politischer Ansichten verwendet. So werden häufig Politiker, ideologisch gefärbte Porträts oder politische Symbole abgebildet. Möglicherweise erfüllen einige aber auch einen ähnlichen Zweck wie die **Tags** in der Hip-Hop-Szene, das heißt die Signatur eines Werkes durch den Künstler; dabei erfährt der Künstler umso mehr Anerkennung, je spektakulärer der Ort gewählt ist. Text wird selten alleine gesprüht, sondern meist nur in Form von einzelnen Wörtern oder Abkürzungen im Werk selbst oder in Bezug auf Darstellungen, die sich in der Nähe befinden.

Stencils

Stencil art *is a form of graffiti done using plates with cut-out shapes. It functions as a kind of open-air screen print and emerged in the 1970s in France (also known as* **pochoirs***). It had its first heyday in the 1980s in Paris.*

Unlike graffiti, however, ***stencil art*** *demands a certain amount of preparation since the* ***stencils*** *must be created in advance. They are usually cardboard, but some are made of plastic or laminated paper. Less common are wood or metal* ***stencils****.* ***Stencils*** *are ideal for creating multiple reproductions of a single motif on streets. Complex and large artifacts are mounted onto all kinds of surfaces. Combining stencils with color allows for an infinite number of possibilities.* ***Stencils*** *are also used to spread political views, for example when they portray politicians, ideologically tainted figures or political symbols. But they can also fulfill a purpose similar to the way* ***tags*** *function in the hip-hop scene – as the signature to an artist's work. The more spectacular the site, the more recognition is paid to the artist. Texts are rarely sprayed alone. They usually appear as isolated words or abbreviations within a work or in reference to other artworks located nearby.*

Dolk

IR

Dolk

Dolk

C215

Dolk

Don John

Gadget

Dolk

Emess

Baumgärtel

Alias

Dolk

We are
free
artists
outside.

FUCK
TM

SMILE
U R ON TV

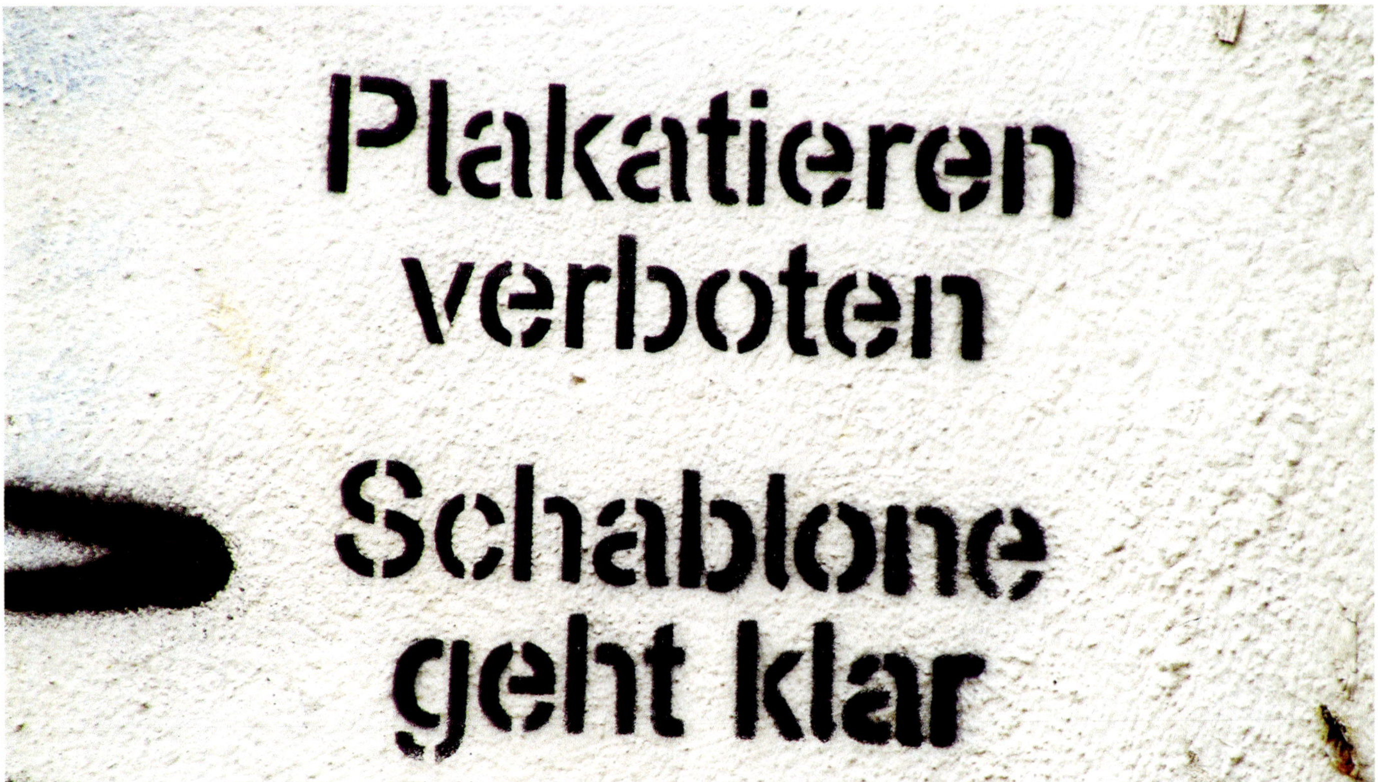
Plakatieren
verboten
Schablone
geht klar

Jimmy C

KREUZBERG
BLEIBT
UNHÖFLICH

CAPITALISM™

Dolk

Ambush

Faile

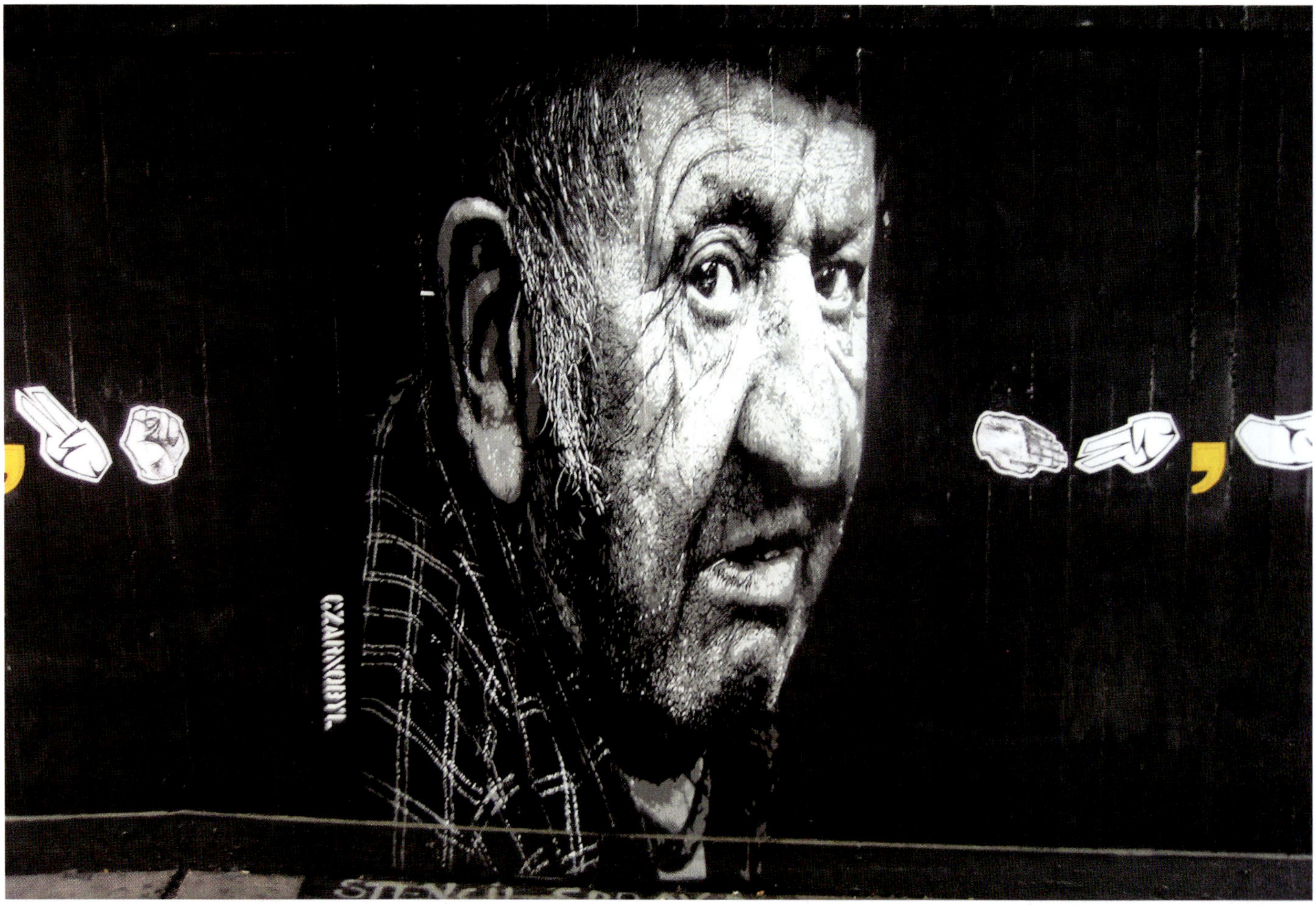

Czarnobyl

Dolk

Various

Paste-ups

Paste-up ist ein Begriff aus der Street-Art-Kultur und meint im Allgemeinen ein mit Kleister oder Leim aufgezogenes Plakat.

Diese Form der Kunst fällt in die Grauzone der Gesetzgebung, da die Plakate meist rückstandsfrei entfernt werden können und somit keine illegale Handlung vorliegt, was auch in der Intention des Künstlers liegt.

Größere **Paste-ups** werden meist durch Siebdruck oder Schablonen hergestellt, kleinere ausgedruckt oder direkt von Hand gezeichnet. Dem Papier wird besondere Beachtung geschenkt, es sollte dicker und stabiler sein als herkömmliches, da es durch die Feuchtigkeit des Klebstoffes beim Aufziehen reißen oder beschädigt werden kann.

Cut-outs

Cut-outs sind im eigentlichen Sinne ausgeschnittene **Paste-ups**. Durch das Herausnehmen des eigentlichen Werkes aus seiner Papierumrahmung entstehen völlig neue Möglichkeiten der Platzierung auf den jeweiligen Untergrundflächen. Im Gegensatz zu einem Plakat, das immer eine rechtwinklige Fläche darstellt, sind **Cut-outs** durch ihre auf das Kunstwerk bezogene Kontur viel einfacher und vielfältiger in die Umgebung zu integrieren.

Stickerart

Stickerart ist eine Form der Street Art, bei der Aufkleber im öffentlichen Raum angebracht werden. Besonders seit Anfang des 21. Jahrhunderts ist diese Erscheinung häufig in Großstädten, beispielsweise auf Mülleimern, Verkehrsschildern oder Hauswänden, zu sehen. Oft bestehen die Werke aus beschrifteten oder bemalten kostenlos erhältlichen Aufklebern. Besonders zu erwähnen sind die bundesweit überaus leicht verfügbaren Aufkleber für Pakete und Päckchen von Postlieferdiensten. Deren sehr gute Klebeeigenschaften erklären ihre große Beliebtheit bei Street-Artisten, die sich wiederum auffällig im Straßenbild niederschlägt. Sticker können preiswert bedruckt oder bemalt werden und sind leichter anzubringen als Graffiti.

Überall kleben die Sticker. Auf unterschiedlichste Art und Weise bearbeitet, sind sie nie langweilig und immer wieder überraschend. Von der Verwendung von Textmarkern oder Schablonengraffiti bis hin zu Siebdruck und dem Aufdruck von Bildern per Computer gibt es unzählige Möglichkeiten der kreativen Entfaltung.

Viele Motive sind gleich mehrmals an verschiedenen Orten, teilweise gleichzeitig in unterschiedlichen Städten, angebracht, um subversiv auf Passanten einzuwirken und in ihrer Präsenz auf die beeinflussende Wirkung der Massenmedien aufmerksam zu machen. Dieser Effekt wurde ebenfalls von der Industrie entdeckt, weshalb mittlerweile verstärkt auch kommerzielle Aufkleber im öffentlichen Raum zu sehen sind.

Im Gegensatz zum Graffito fällt diese Form der Straßenkunst nicht unter den Strafbestand der Sachbeschädigung, sondern gilt als Wildplakatierung; damit stellt es, genauso wie **Paste-ups**, „nur" eine Ordnungswidrigkeit dar.

Paste-Ups

__Paste-up__ is a term from street art culture and refers in general to a poster hung with glue or paste.

This kind of art falls into a legal grey area since posters can usually be removed without leaving behind any residue or damage. Hanging posters, therefore, is not a criminal act, nor does the artist want it to be.

Larger __paste-ups__ are usually produced with screen prints or stencils. Smaller ones are printed or drawn by hand. Artists give special care to the paper they use. It has to be thicker and more stable then regular paper since the moist glue makes it easy to tear or damage when hung.

Cut-Outs

__Cut-outs__ are actually cut out __paste-ups.__ Removing the actual work from its paper framework allows it to be placed on any number of different surfaces. Unlike a poster that is always rectangular, the shape of the __cut-outs__ is determined by the work of art and can be more easily and diversely integrated into the environment.

Sticker Art

__Sticker art__ is a form of street art in which sticky labels are displayed in public space. This trend has become increasingly popular in large cities in the 21st century. The stickers can be found on trash cans, traffic signs and building fronts. They are usually pre-printed or adapted into colored stickers from free self-sealing labels. The self-selling labels used to send packages by postal delivery services and which are easily available throughout Germany deserve special mention. Their high-quality sealing glue makes them very popular among street artists and explains why they are so often seen on the streets. Stickers are inexpensive to print and color and are easier than graffiti to apply.

The stickers, created and designed in very different ways, are pasted everywhere. They are never dull and continually surprising. Be it through the use of highlighters, stencil graffiti, screen prints or pictures printed from a computer, the artists find an infinite number of ways to develop their creativity.

You will often find the same motif pasted at different locations, sometimes even in different cities, at the same time. The aim is to achieve a subversive impact on passersby and to draw attention to the influence of mass media. The media industry has also discovered this method, which is why you will also find an increase in commercial stickers in public spaces.

Unlike graffiti, this form of street art does not qualify as property damage. __Sticker art__ forms are regarded as illegal placards and like __paste-ups__ they qualify "only" as a misdemeanor.

JS

Swoon

Various & Gould

Urben

Icy and Sot

Marek

Alias

Various & Gould

Linda's Ex

Karl Toon; Tower

NoLogo

Kurar

Chunko

Blo

C215

Alias

Bronco

Solovei

Christian Paine

Alias

Eddek

Fvol

Pank

IT IS
Achtung
SCHÖNEBL..G
Verlangerung!
16
KOOL
mitte
LUFT UND
LAUNE
OR 23.
IT IS
QUIT NOW
ATM
BAD

HAMBURG
TERRORIST
PIGALLE

Swoon

Bronco

Prost

Tower

Boxi

Primo

Alle Bilder / all pictures: Swoon

Alle Bilder/all pictures: Swoon

Jakob

Gould

Tower

Christian Paine

Stroke, El Bocho

Tower

Rero

Gould

Tower

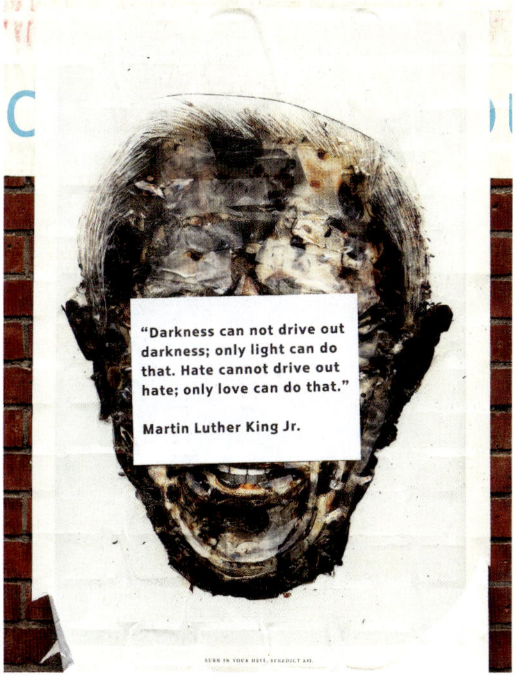

Alias

Wurstbande

Alias

§ 23

WAHREN SIE IHRE RECHTE ALS KONSUMENT!

Swoon

DUBON
H100

LIMP.H
RUSSE

Alias

Base 23

Mentalgassi

Alias

FOR THE
Times
THEY ARE
A CHANGING
KKADE

hat der Berliner keene
Verpeilung
sagt er seinem Boss
seine „Meinung"

Eddek

Joska

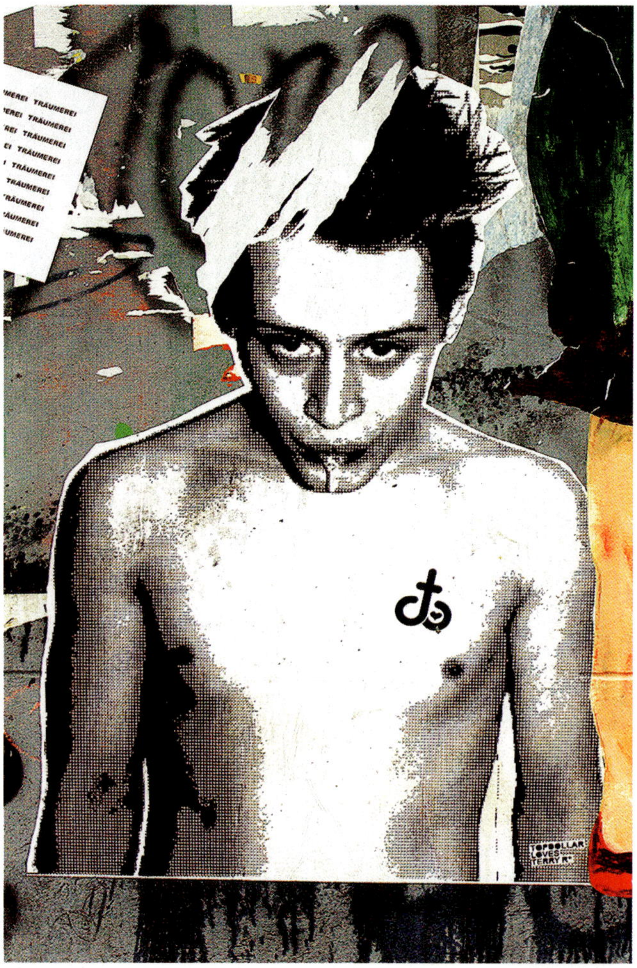

Alias

Miss Riehl

Soon

Mimi The Clown

Eddek

Direkter Farbauftrag

Hierbei handelt es sich um das Auftragen von Farbe auf den Untergrund ohne weitere Hilfsmittel, also das direkte Bemalen mit Pinsel, Spraydose oder beispielsweise auch mit Textmarker. Im Gegensatz zu anderen Techniken, bei denen die Werke vorbereitet werden können und die dann vor Ort nur noch angebracht werden müssen, erfordert diese Technik relativ viel Zeit und Ruhe. Das beeinflusst natürlich auch die Wahl des Ortes, da man nicht an jedem Ort so frei arbeiten kann, wie es nötig ist. Es verhält sich hier ähnlich wie bei großen und aufwendigen Graffiti-Pieces. Umso mehr muss man die Leistung anerkennen, wenn ein Künstler es schafft, ein technisch umfangreiches und gleichzeitig anmutendes Werk an einem repräsentativen Ort zu erschaffen. Die Wände mutieren dabei zu einer steinernen Leinwand. Dies ist vielleicht die am engsten mit der klassischen Malerei verwandte Technik der Street Art.

Direct Application of Paint

Here it is a question of applying paint directly onto the image carrier without any preparatory measures, meaning painting or drawing directly onto a surface with a paintbrush, a can of spray paint or a permanent text marker. In contrast to other techniques with which works can be prepared and then only need to be mounted on site, such a technique requires ample and time composure, which naturally plays a role in choosing where to execute a work since not all locations provide the freedom necessary to create such art. This is similar to cases of large and elaborate graffiti works. Such achievements should be recognized all the more when an artist is able to create a technically complicated and simultaneously striking work in a prestigious location. The walls are hereby transformed into stone canvases. This is perhaps the technique in Street Art that is most closely related to classical painting.

El Bocho

Nomad

MTO

Kola @ Urban Affairs Extended 2009

Kowalski

Sam 3

Otto Schade

Rubin, Mymo

Jimmy C

Mto

COOKED

M-City

M.R.P.
BAR
www.akajimm

Jimmy C

ERROR
ZOFF
KUKUK
SMIL

SGS
MTO
ALIAS

××2009×1986××××
×××
UGLY
AS
NA
TU
RE
××××
××××
×××× NOMAD ×× JUS

Marek @ Urban Affairs Extended 2009

Sam 3

Roa

Broken Fingaz

1010 @ Urbain Affairs Extended 2009

Nomad

Milda

Nomad

Otto Schade

M City, Zbiok, Czarnobyl

Kowalski

Kraser

Murals

Gerade in den Bezirken Kreuzberg und Wedding findet man immer häufiger bunte, kreativ bearbeitete Wandflächen. Als Untergrund für die Kunstwerke dienen die vielfach in der ganzen Stadt auftauchenden kahlen und grauen Brandwände. Brandwände sind Zeugen der Zerstörung der Häuserreihen durch Krieg, pleitegegangener Bauvorhaben oder stadtplanerischer Fehltritte. Und auch wenn sie fest zum Berliner Stadtbild gehören, wirken sie noch lange nicht freundlich. Um dem entgegenzuwirken und um immer neue kreative Akzente in der Stadt zu setzen, werden regelmäßig im Rahmen von lokalen Street-Art-Events – zunächst „Backjumps" und später auch „Urban Grassroots: Planet Prozess", „Urban Affairs", „Wedding Walls" oder „Urban Nations" – bekannte Street-Art-Künstler eingeladen, den Kiez mit ihrer Kunst zu verschönern und optisch aufzuwerten. Die Kunstwerke integrieren sich nicht nur, sie werden zur Sehenswürdigkeit. Hier erfährt der öffentliche Raum einen Eingriff, der harmonisch funktioniert und bereichernd wirkt. Die Kunst unterstreicht ihre Umgebung, einen multikulturellen Kiez mit besonderem Charme und aufgeschlossenen Menschen. Erwähnenswert bleibt die Tatsache, dass die Gestaltung der Brandwände einvernehmlich erfolgt und nicht gegen den Willen der Obrigkeit – ein gutes Beispiel für die Akzeptanz der Street Art in der Öffentlichkeit und eine Freude für den Betrachter.

Murals

*The number of colorful, creative **murals** found in the Kreuzberg and Wedding districts is growing rapidly. The city's many bare, grey building fire walls serve as a canvas for the artwork. Fire walls are a reminder of how war, bankrupt building projects or failed urban planning can destroy a block of houses. And although they are an established part of the Berlin cityscape, the fire walls are not particularly attractive. In order to change this and to set new creative accents, street artists are often invited – in connection with local street art events (first "Backjumps" and later also "Urban Grassroots: Planet Prozess", "Urban Affairs", "Wedding Walls" and "Urban Nations") – to beautify the neighborhood and enhance it visually with their art. The artwork is not only integrated into the environment, it actually becomes an attraction. In this case the public space is encroached upon in a harmonious way which serves as an added improvement to the neighborhood. The art punctuates its surroundings – in the case of Kreuzberg, a multi-cultural neighborhood with a special charm and friendly, open people. It is worth mentioning that the design of fire walls takes place under amicable circumstances and is tolerated by the public authorities. This is a good example for the public acceptance of street art and the pleasure it brings to the viewer.*

Blu

at the Beach
JEDEN FREITAG
METAXA BAY

Superblast

The London Police

TOMCAT
PEREZ
T.O.P.K.
FRESH
TAPE

2008
100 EURO

Ima Village

Superblast

YOGA
MOPLAK
Mitte
geschmackvoll
Made in Berlin
4m

Ash @ Wedding Walls

KROK

Ash

Os Gemeos

Icy and Sot

Blo

Kobe, AgeAge, Roa

INTERBRIGADAS

Grafro and others ... by Interbrigadas

Shepard Fairy @ One Wall/Urban Nation

Don Jon @ One Wall/Urban Nation

Karl Addison & James Bullough @ Wedding Walls

Nomad

Tristan Eaton @ One Wall/Urban Nation

Twoone @ Urban Nation

Project/M von Urban Nation
Urban Nation ist eine Plattform für Kunstprojekte mit dem Fokus auf Street Art. Mit dem Ziel, durch Kunst den urbanen Lebensraum zu gestalten, um so einen höheren Lebenswert für die Gemeinschaft generieren zu können, bringt Urban Nation Künstler mittels unterschiedlicher Projekte in eine Kommunikationssituation zueinander und in den Dialog mit der Öffentlichkeit. Mit Project/M werden mehrmals im Jahr besondere Künstler dazu eingeladen, die Fassade des Hauses in der Bülowstraße zu gestalten. Hier dazu drei hervorragende Beispiele:

Project/M by Urban Nation
Urban Nation is a platform for art projects that focus on Street Art. It designs urban space with art as a way to make it more livable for the community. Urban Nation artists bring different projects together so that they can communicate and engage in a dialogue with the public. As part of Project/M, special artists are invited several times a year to design the façade of the building on Bülowstrasse. Here are three exceptional examples:

Handiedan und Dalest

Dabs Myla

Rone

Husk mit Navn

NoMAD
GENUG GESPART!
Fußball
Boxen
Football
Basketball
Formel 1
Radsport
Eishockey
HAPPYBet
Nomad

Roa

FFEE

Bio @ Wedding Walls

El Bocho's Tape-Art-Weltrekord!
Der Berliner Künstler El Bocho beklebte im Jahr 2009 im Rahmen der Ausstellung „Urban Affairs Extended" nur mit Klebestreifen die Wand des Stadtbad Wedding. Tape Art ist eine Kunsttechnik, von der man in Zukunft noch viel sehen wird.

***El Bocho's** Tape Art world record!*
Within the scope of the exhibition "Urban Affairs Extended" in 2009, the Berlin artist El Bocho covered a wall of the public swimming pool in Wedding using nothing more than tape. Tape Art is an artistic technique that we will see a great deal more of in the future.

Andere Techniken

Neben den weitverbreiteten Techniken wie beispielsweise **Paste-up**, **Stencil** oder auch **Cut-out** gibt es eine Vielzahl weiterer Möglichkeiten, wie sich die Künstler ins Straßenbild einbringen können. Zum einen ist da die Installation von Objekten, welche entweder an einem anderen Ort vorgefertigt und dann installiert werden oder direkt „on location" entstehen. Hierbei gibt es bei Umsetzung und Material keine Grenzen. Dazu kommen weitere Möglichkeiten wie beispielsweise **Decollage** (das Abtragen von übereinanderliegenden Schichten, um Formen entstehen zu lassen), **Scratchiti** (das Einkratzen in harte Oberflächen), **Tape Art** (das Aufbringen von Klebestreifen), **Tile Board** (das Anbringen von Kunstwerken auf stabilem Trägermaterial), **Kreidezeichnung**, **Ad-Busting** (das Verändern von Werbeplakaten), **Urban Knitting** (das Einfassen von Gegenständen mit Strickware), elektronische Umsetzungen mittels **LED-Technik** oder **Videoprojektion** sowie **Folierung** (das Anbringen und/oder Einwickeln von Gegenständen im Straßenraum mit Frischhaltefolie) und sicher noch einige mehr. Diese Vielzahl an Optionen macht den urbanen Raum nahezu vollständig erschließbar für die Street Art, welche theoretisch dem Künstler alle Möglichkeiten eröffnet, sich im öffentlichen Raum zu positionieren.

Other Techniques

*In addition to widely used techniques such as **paste-up**, **stencil** and **cut-outs**, there are a number of other ways for artists to participate in street life. There is, for example, the installation of objects which are either created elsewhere and later installed at the site or which are created right "on location." The methods and materials used to execute these different techniques are infinite. A variety of methods include **decollage** (removing overlapping layers to allow forms to emerge), **scratchiti** (scratching into hard surfaces), **tape art** (sticking adhesive tape), **tile board** (putting artwork onto a stable base), **chalk drawings**, **ad busting** (altering poster ads), **urban knitting** (wrapping objects with yarn), electronic light presentations using **LED technology** or **video projection** and **plastic wrapping** (fastening or wrapping objects on the street using cling wrap) and probably quite a few others. With so many different options, almost all urban space becomes accessible to street art, providing artists with endless ways to position themselves in public space.*

Clemens Behr @ Stroke Art Fair

GUTEN TAG BERLIN !

RECLAIM YOUR CITY.NET

Christiaan Nagel

Nomad

SABA

MEDIASPREE
MEDIASPREE

BURIED IN
CONCRETE
Simply the best

FRAU
REIDL

6@artist

Chinagirl & Dan Kitchener

Ines Tartler

URBAN
ART
CLASH
BOSSO
FATAKA
loves
yellow

Tower

El Bocho

Straßenkunst gehört zum Stadtbild, und es gibt Städte, wie zum Beispiel London, Tokio und Berlin, deren Einwohner ihre Stadtkünstler richtig feiern, weil sie sich mit den Werken im Straßenbild identifizieren können. Eigentlich ist es leicht, einen guten Street-Artisten auszumachen.

Man kann das gut am Beispiel des aus Frankfurt nach Berlin zugezogenen **El Bocho** beschreiben. Er sucht sich Berliner Orte aus, an denen er die Betrachter seiner Werke begrüßt, mit „Breakfast in Berlin", „Colour the City", „Berlin", „Ich sehe was, was Du nicht siehst". Seine Straßenbilder sind anregend, geben ein gutes Gefühl mit auf den Weg und beschwingen den Schritt des Weitergehenden ebenso, wie sie dessen Gedanken beflügeln. Die Überraschung, auf dem Weg durch die Stadt einem seiner Werke begegnet zu sein, ist nicht zu überbieten. Dabei ist ihm wichtig, durch seine Werke nicht direkt ins Stadtbild einzugreifen, sondern es zu ergänzen und zu verändern: Er arbeitet nicht direkt auf der Mauer, sondern bereitet seine Werke auf braunem Packpapier vor, das er nur noch an der richtigen Stelle an Wänden befestigt. Als wolle er sagen, hier kann es schöner sein, die Stimmung gehoben, habt ihr darüber einmal nachgedacht? Und wenn man wieder einmal als Bummler durch dieselbe Straße geht, ist das Bild längst fort, aber die Erinnerung daran bleibt.

El Bocho ist für Berlin ein Glücksfall. Man sagt von Berlin, dass hier die Vergangenheit immer noch auf der Straße liege. **El Bocho** schärft den Blick auf Relikte in der Stadt und Erinnerungen aufregender oder anrührender Momente. Er setzt Zeichen, die der Betrachter wiedererkennt, nicht etwa mit dem Zeigefinger, auch nicht durch Kritik am Zustand mancher Ecken. Es ist etwas Neues, das durch seine Gemälde sichtbar wird, es schafft ein wenig ephemere Schönheit und weist damit gleichzeitig auf die Vergänglichkeit allen Strebens hin. **El Bocho** ist ein Romantiker ... und das passt sehr gut nach Berlin.

Street art is a part of the city's appearance, and in some cities, such as London, Tokyo and Berlin, the residents celebrate their city artists because they are able to identify with their work on the streets. It is actually quite easy to recognize a good street artist.

El Bocho*, who moved from Frankfurt to Berlin, is a good example: He looks for sites in Berlin where he can greet observers of his works with "Breakfast in Berlin," "Colour the City," "Berlin" or "I see something that you don't see." His street paintings are stimulating and make people feel good as they pass by, causing them to lift their pace while firing their imagination. It is always a great surprise to encounter one of his works while going through the city. It is important to him that his works don't interfere with the cityscape, but rather add to and alter it. He does not work directly on the wall but instead prepares his work beforehand on brown packaging paper that he then fastens to the right place on a wall. It's as if he wants to say: "This could be prettier here, lifting spirits, have you ever thought about that?" And the next time you saunter along this street, the picture is long gone, but the memory of it remains.*

El Bocho *is a stroke of luck for Berlin. It is said that the past still lies on the street in Berlin.* ***El Bocho*** *makes people more aware of the relics in the city and sharpens the memory of exciting and moving moments. He creates symbols that the observer recognizes, but the artist doesn't point his finger admonishingly or criticize the condition of certain areas. His paintings make something new become visible. They create a little ephemeral beauty while at the same time pointing out how transitory all aspirations are.* ***El Bocho*** *is a romantic and that fits Berlin very well.*

ICH HABE SEHNSUCHT, DOCH WEIß ICH NICHT WONACH..
EL BOCHO

MANCHMAL SEH ICH LIEBE WO GARKEINE IST.
BOCHO BERLIN
SOIRÉE

LITTLE LUCY
08

LITTLE LUCY
WELCOME TO BERLIN
EL BOCHO
Live in Concert
Songs of the Soul
The Music of Sri Chinmoy
Mo 2. Juni 20°°
Admiralspalast

BRAUCH ICH DEN GANZEN MIST WIRKLICH ???
30

Auguststraße

EL BOCHO
LITTLE LUCY
KILKENNY
IN EXTREMO

EL BOCHO

C'EST LA VIE
sunshine cleaning
ELDORADO
I ♥ GOLD

EL BOCHO

...DIE KÜSSE UNTER DER KELLERTREPPE MEINES PLATTENBAUS.
EL BOCHO

HEY TOURIST. GERMAN LESSON 1:
KOMM ICH SO INS WATERGATE ?
TINA BERLINA
B
EL BOCHO

LITTLE LUCY
..DIE KITTI.
ÄHH, DER
FROSCH IST
DOOF!

EL BOCHO

EL BOCHO
"DIE SIEDLUNG IST MY WONDERLAND"
17 PM
Open Air Sommertheater
24 Juli - 5 August

EL BOCHO BERLIN

JR

Der französische Fotograf und Künstler **JR** erregte schon vor einigen Jahren großes Aufsehen in Berlin mit seinem großformatigen Paste-up-Projekt „Face2Face", das er an Hauswänden am Checkpoint Charlie anbrachte.

Anfang 2013 war **JR** erneut in der Stadt und hat viele Wände im gesamten Stadtgebiet gestaltet – dieses Mal mit seinem Projekt „The Wrinkles of the City", mit dem er zuvor bereits Shanghai, Los Angeles, Havanna und Cartagena bespielt hat.

In „The Wrinkles of the City" geht es um die Zeit, um die Sichtbarmachung der Vergangenheit und des Jetzt. **JR**s großformatige Paste-ups zeigen Porträts von alten Berlinern, also Menschen, die eine lange Vergangenheit hinter sich haben. Vielleicht haben sie den Krieg, die Teilung der Stadt, die Wendezeit miterlebt, Tragödien und Glücksfälle erfahren. Es sind Menschen, deren faltige Haut und deren Augen eine stille Geschichte erzählen, deren Gesichtszüge und Narben zur biographischen Landkarte geworden sind. Angebracht an Wänden von Häusern, deren Mauern und Oberflächen ebenfalls in ihrer Textur eine lange Geschichte zu erzählen haben, gehen diese Porträts eine Symbiose mit dem Gemäuer ein. Beide vermitteln gemeinsam den Lauf der Zeit, das bereits Geschehene und das Jetzt. Und das Ende ist für den Ort wie auch den Menschen unabdingbar dasselbe, sie sind, genau wie **JR**s Kunstwerke, der Vergänglichkeit preisgegeben.

Dabei erfahren die Menschen wie auch die Orte eine Würdigung durch **JR**, sucht er sie doch bewusst aus und wird dabei niemals anmaßend. Gerade Berlin scheint ideal für „The Wrinkles of the City": Diese „immer werdende, niemals fertige Stadt" hat eine sehr bewegte Vergangenheit, und die Wände der Stadt haben Narben. Die urbane Konfiguration der Stadt ist Flickwerk aus vielen Jahrzehnten einschneidender historischer Ereignisse. Ereignisse, die auch die Menschen der Stadt mit sich tragen.

__JR__, the French photographer and artist, caused a sensation in Berlin a few years back with his large-size paste-up project "Face2Face" that he put on the walls of buildings at Checkpoint Charlie.

In early 2013 when __JR__ was in Berlin again he designed a lot of walls throughout the city – this time with his project "The Wrinkles of the City" that he had previously tried out in Shanghai, Los Angeles, Havanna und Cartagena.

"The Wrinkles of the City" is about time and making the present and the past visible. __JR__'s large size paste-ups portray old Berliners, people who have a long past behind them. Maybe they lived through the war, or the division of the city, experienced the fall of the Berlin Wall, endured tragedies or enjoyed good fortune. These are people whose wrinkly skin and eyes tell a quiet story, whose facial features and scars have become a biological map. They are placed on the walls of buildings whose texture and surfaces also have a long story to tell. The portraits form a symbiosis with the masonry. Together they convey the passage of time, depicting things that have already happened as well as what is going on in the present. Like with people, a place must also inevitably come to an end. Like __JR__'s artwork, they too are vulnerable to impermanence.

Through his work these people and places receive positive attention. He selects them carefully, but is never arrogant. Berlin seems to be the ideal place for "The Wrinkles of the City": This "ever-changing never-finished city" had a very vibrant history and its walls bear its scars. The urban configuration of Berlin is a patchwork formed by many years of dramatic historical events – events that have also left their imprint on the people who live here.

GALERIA

54
SIMON

EISERN
UNION!

Rosenthaler Straße

APOTHEKE
NORDLAND
APOTHEKE

KUNST YOUR-SELF

SP 38

Berlin Mitte ist vielleicht der Bezirk, der sich in den letzten Jahren am meisten gewandelt hat. Die grauen, brüchigen Fassaden der Nachwendezeit sind durch renovierte Häuser und moderne Neubauten ersetzt worden; statt Leerstand gibt es etablierte Ladengeschäfte. Die Kunstszene hat sich durch diesen Gentrifizierungsprozess ebenso stark verändert, sie ist nicht mehr so ungebunden und radikal wie zuvor, und auch die ansässigen Galerien bedienen nun eine andere Zielgruppe.

SP 38 ist einer der Protagonisten der früheren Tage und lebt noch immer in seiner alten Umgebung. Mittels seines künstlerischen Ausdrucks, des großen Plakates mit Schriftzug, kommentiert er seit vielen Jahren in kurzen Statements den Wandel des Viertels. Seine Art, die Schriftzüge zu gestalten, und die dafür genutzten Farben sind unverkennbar. Ein Plakat von **SP 38** ist so charakteristisch, dass es inzwischen durchaus als Label funktioniert.

So sieht man beim Spaziergang durch Mitte unzählige seiner Kommentare an den Wänden und Mauern: Mit „who kills Mitte?" hinterfragt er die Protagonisten der Gentrifikation, der Ausruf „vive la bourgeoisie" ironisiert die neuen Bewohner von Mitte, „i don't wanna be ur friend on facebook" kann als Kritik an der „Bussi-Bussi-Gesellschaft" und deren Oberflächlichkeit gelesen werden.

Diese und viele weitere Slogans sind aber keinesfalls als Wutausbruch eines Ewig-Gestrigen zu verstehen, sondern mehr als eine Art erinnernder Weckruf, der nicht vergessen lassen will, dass die Effekte von Kommerz, Verdrängung und Unisexifizierung von Lebensräumen durchaus zu hinterfragen sind. Somit ist **SP 38** vielleicht der Protagonist der Berliner Street-Art-Szene, dessen Arbeit am engsten mit seiner Umgebung verbunden ist und am deutlichsten den Urgedanken der Street-Art repräsentiert: die „Rückeroberung der Straße".

Berlin Mitte is probably the district that underwent the most change over the last years. The grey, crumbling building fronts that were seen everywhere in the years after the Wall fell have been replaced by newly-renovated buildings and modern new structures. Vacant store fronts are now occupied by successful shops. The art scene was also strongly altered by the process of gentrification. It is no longer as detached and radical as it once was and the established galleries now play to a different audience.

SP 38 *is one of the protagonists from an earlier time who still lives in his old surroundings. For many years he has been commenting on the changes in his neighborhood through his choice of artistic expression – the large poster with brief statements. The design of his posters – his lettering and the colors he uses – is unmistakable.* ***SP 38****'s posters are so characteristic of his work that they could even function as a label.*

Walking through Mitte one finds his comments on various walls and building fronts. He poses the question to the protagonists of gentrification: "who kills Mitte?" His appeal "vive la bourgeoisie" is an ironic reference to the new residents of Mitte. "i don't wanna be ur friend on facebook" can be understood as a criticism of the "in-crowd" and the shallowness it represents.

These and many other slogans should not be misconstrued as the anger of someone hanging onto the good ol' days. They are more like a friendly wake-up call reminding us that we should continue to question the way that commerce, displacement and unisexification affects our living space. In this sense ***SP 38*** *is probably the central player in the Berlin Street Art scene whose work is most closely connected to the area that he lives in. Hence he best represents the original idea behind Street Art: "Reclaim the streets".*

MADE IN DREAM

Auguststraße
CHARLIE !

KIEZ ME
BERLIN DAILY
EDITIONSGALERIE
FÜR PHOTOJOUR
NALISMUS
OCCUPY THE SKY

ESCAPE

NoMo
NEY N
o Art

WHo KILLS
THE CoM
MISSIoN.

ESC4P
E FRoM
IMMoNEY
IMMODELFIN.COM

WHOKILLSMITTE?
AGAIN
reMMX
Jeongmoon Choi

FUMEDUPNEU

231
ESCAPE
TOURIS TA GO HOME!
BERLIN IS A B ITCH!
TOURIS TA GO HOME!
TOURIS TA GO HOME!
BERLIN IS A B EACH!
BERLIN IS A B ITCH!
TOURIS TA GO HOME!
BERLIN IS A B ITCH!

Emess

Emess erforscht seit nunmehr über einem Jahrzehnt intensiv die Gestaltungsmöglichkeiten und Wirkungsweisen des öffentlichen Raumes. Mittels künstlerischer Irritationsmomente und urbaner Interventionen strebt **Emess** danach, gewohnte Überzeugungen zu hinterfragen und neue Denkprozesse anzustoßen. Durch irritierende oder provokative Sujets sucht **Emess** die Aufmerksamkeit der Öffentlichkeit zu erregen und greift dabei nur zu gern lokale Problematiken auf, die eine globale Relevanz haben.

Emess' Arbeiten sind häufig durch politische Fragen motiviert. Er konfrontiert den Betrachter mit Problemen, die sonst eher unter den Teppich gekehrt würden oder für die es möglicherweise keine klaren Antworten oder Lösungen gibt. Humor und Sinn für Ästhetik überraschen den Betrachter und lenken die Aufmerksamkeit auf den Inhalt seiner Arbeiten. **Emess** macht keinen Unterschied zwischen öffentlichem Raum und Galerie, seine Arbeiten sind konzipiert, um ein Publikum zu erreichen, und passen sich der jeweiligen Situation an. Die Bandbreite seines Schaffens erstreckt sich dabei von Skulpturen und Installationen über großformatige Wandmalereien und Plakatierungen bis hin zu filigranen Holzschnitten und farbstarken Drucken.

*For more than a decade now, **Emess** has been intensively exploring different ways to design and influence public space. Through artistic moments of irrationality and urban intervention, **Emess** strives to question accepted beliefs and inspire new thought processes. With jarring or provocative subjects, **Emess** seeks to arouse public attention, taking pleasure in addressing local problems that have global relevance.*

***Emess'** work is often motivated by political issues. He confronts the viewer with problems that are often swept under the carpet or which have no clear answers or solutions. His humor and aesthetic sense surprise the observer and draw attention back to the content of his work. **Emess** does not distinguish between public space and gallery – his works are designed to reach a public and adapt to the different situations. His creations cover a broad span ranging from sculpture and installations to large wall murals and posters, extending to delicate wood carvings and deeply colorful prints.*

WATCH
YOUR
HEAD
EMESS

..DONT MATTER TONIGHT!

WATCH
YOUR
HEAD

EAT THE
RICH

Why not ?

O2
..can't buy
me love!

41
Ich kann gar
nicht soviel
essen, wie
ich kotzen
möchte..

Vhils

Alexandre Farto aka **Vhils** ist im heutigen urbanen Kunstgeschehen besonders hervorzuheben. Denn er setzt auf spektakuläre Art und Weise genau das um, was das Wort Graffiti etymologisch eigentlich bedeutet: Schrift in Stein einzuritzen.

Der aus Lissabon stammende **Vhils** studierte in London Kunst und Design und beschäftigt sich in seiner künstlerischen Arbeit fast schon wie ein Archäologe mit dem Freilegen historischer Schichten. Ob Holz, Stein, Papier oder Metall – **Vhils** ringt dem Material mit unterschiedlichen Techniken, beispielsweise mit dem Meißel, mit Säure oder mit Sprengstoff, Schicht für Schicht seine Oberfläche ab und schafft so durch Zerstörung etwas Neues. Er dringt ein in die Vergangenheit des Untergrundes und legt so das Dahinter frei. Gleichzeitig schafft er ein Kunstwerk und macht seine urbane Spielfläche selbst zum Medium. Dabei zeigt er Porträts lokaler Personen, welche er durch seine Arbeit in die Oberflächen ihrer Lebensräume implantiert. So werden die Bewohner der Stadt selbst zu deren architektonischem Gesicht, die Stadt wird zum Spiegelbild der Menschen, die sie prägen.

Vhils beweist, dass durch Dekonstruktion und Zerstörung Neues erschaffen werden kann. Nur etwas, das sich verändert, das vergänglich ist, kann Raum schaffen für neue Prozesse und so den Stillstand aufheben. Neue Möglichkeiten entstehen, wenn alte Strukturen aufgebrochen werden. Auch die Kunst von **Vhils** ist zeitlich begrenzt: Häuser werden abgerissen, Wände überdeckt, Kunstwerke verwittern und verschwinden. So funktioniert Street Art, durch ihre ephemere Form nimmt sie sich kurz Raum, um ihn dann wieder freizugeben für etwas Neues.

Vhils sieht in der aktuellen Diskussion um die Rolle der urbanen Kunst im White Cube des Ausstellungsbetriebs keinen Widerspruch zwischen Galerie und direktem, unvermitteltem Arbeiten auf der Straße. Sein Erfolg zeigt, wie man in beiden Disziplinen bestehen und trotzdem glaubwürdig sein kann.

*Alexandre Farto aka **Vhils** deserves special mention in today's urban art scene. In a spectacular way, he does exactly what the etymological sense of the word "graffiti" actually means: carving writing into stone.*

***Vhils**, who originally comes from Lisbon, studied art and design in London. In his artistic work, he acts like an archaeologist excavating layers of history. Whether it is wood, stone, paper or metal, **Vhils** uses different techniques – a chisel or acid or explosives – to remove the surface of the material layer by layer. Through this act of destruction he creates something new. He penetrates the past deep underground and reveals what is lying behind it. At the same time he creates a work of art and even turns his urban playing area into a medium. He shows portraits of local figures which he implants into the surface of their living space, making the residents of the city a part of its architecture. The city becomes a reflection of the people that have shaped it.*

***Vhils** demonstrates that through destruction and deconstruction something new can be created. But it is something that changes, that is transient, that can create space for new processes and eliminate stagnancy. New possibilities arise when old structures are broken up. Vhils' art too is temporal: buildings are torn down, walls covered over, artwork weathers and disappears. That is how Street Art functions: through its ephemeral form it occupies space temporarily before making it available again for something new.*

*In the current discussion around the role of urban art in the White Cube of exhibition operations **Vhils** does not see a contradiction between galleries and the unexpected works found on the streets. His success shows that it is possible to coexist in both disciplines and still maintain credibility.*

GO FORTH

GO FORTH

GO FORTH
NORDSEE
Die Alternative.
NORDSEE
Die Alternative.
Jeder Kronkorken ein Gewinn!
GEMEINSAM GEHT MEHR.
SNOW WHITE AND THE HUNTSMAN
30
ZONE

GO FORTH
„Every step you tak
contains love

GO FORTH

XOOOOX

Der Street-Art-Künstler **XOOOOX** bringt seit dem Jahre 2001 seine Schablonen und Poster in das Stadtbild mit ein, meist auf heruntergekommenen oder zumindest abgenutzten Untergrundflächen. Eine gewisse Ästhetik ist seinen Werken keinesfalls abzusprechen. Meist empfindet man bei ihrem Betrachten, dass sie im von der breiten Masse tolerierten Normbereich den öffentlichen Raum schmücken, gefördert von der Art und Weise, wie sie an den ausgesuchten Orten bewusst angebracht wurden. Man könnte durchaus zu dem Schluss kommen, es handele sich um Werbung, beispielsweise für ein Modelabel. Gerade in der letzten Zeit bedienen sich tatsächlich mehr und mehr Konzerne und deren Marken der Nachahmung von Street Art als Werbemittel. Doch ist dies bei **XOOOOX** eben nicht der Fall. Es bleibt für den Betrachter eher offen, um was es sich handelt, das Werk nimmt aber im gleichen Atemzug die Nutzung des Mediums Street Art als Werbemittel ironisch aufs Korn. Dabei ist die Schreibweise von **XOOOOX** förderlich, da man die Bestandteile drehen, spiegeln oder zerstückelt ausrichten kann. Der Schriftzug behält dennoch einen hohen Wiedererkennungswert. Wie bei vielen Street-Art-Künstlern ist die gesamte Gestaltung darauf ausgerichtet, trotzdem bleibt die Ausführung vielseitig. **XOOOOX** ist inzwischen auch als Galeriekünstler sehr erfolgreich.

*The street artist **XOOOOX** first introduced his **stencils** and posters to the streets of Berlin in 2001, usually on decaying or worn-out surfaces. There can be no doubt that his work possesses a certain aesthetic. People who observe his work often agree that it is an adornment of public space within the norm tolerated by the broader population. This impression is reinforced by the way in which the artist places his creations at selected sites. They could be mistaken for an advertisement or a design label. Recently, big companies and their major labels have begun to imitate street art in their advertising. But this is not what **XOOOOX** is doing. His work remains ambiguous to viewers, but it is also an ironic attack on the use of the street art medium for advertising. The lettering of **XOOOOX** is also a positive aspect of the presentation since it can be turned around, mirrored or broken apart, but always remains immediately recognizable. Like so much street art, this is one aim of the overall design, but the presentation still remains eclectic. **XOOOOX** is now a very successful gallery artist as well.*

Feuerwehrzufahrt

Aufzug
F

XOOOOX
PARIS

ROGUE

Baustellen
einfahrt

SALE

XOOOOX
GENEVE
S Gas

XOOOOX
PARIS

JUST

Wer durch Berlin läuft und den Kopf gen Himmel streckt, der sieht zwangsläufig die großen Schriftzüge, die oft weit oben an Hauswänden aufgetragen wurden. Und nicht weniger selten kommt es vor, dass einer davon den Namen **JUST** trägt. Man fragt sich, wie die riesigen Buchstaben an diesen scheinbar unerreichbaren Stellen aufgetragen werden konnten. Die Antwort heißt **Roll-On-Technik**. **Roll-Ons** werden mit breiten Malerrollen und Farbe umgesetzt. Das gewährleistet ein schnelles und vor allem großflächiges Auftragen der Farbe. Will man höher hinaus – oder, wenn man vom Dach aus arbeitet, eben tiefer –, dann verlängert man einfach den dazugehörigen Arbeitsstab und kann so die vorher nicht zu erreichende Fläche bearbeiten.

JUST stammt ursprünglich aus dem Ruhrgebiet und lebte und studierte vor seinem Umzug nach Berlin für längere Zeit in Edinburgh. Seine ersten Gehversuche in der urbanen Kunst unternahm er bereits in der fünften und sechsten Klasse, als er sich mit **Graffiti** auseinandersetzte. Die Hip-Hop-bezogene Graffiti-Kultur gab **Just** ein Forum, in dem er sich ausdrücken konnte. Doch mit der Zeit wurden ihm das „Name-Writing" und das Crew-bezogene „Taggen" zu egoistisch, und so fand er den Weg zu einer bildhafteren Darstellung. Zwischen 1999 und ca. 2002 waren es erst nur Plakate und Aufkleber mit antikapitalistischen, antisexistischen oder antifaschistischen Inhalten, später kamen dann viele andere gängige Methoden der Street Art hinzu, unter anderem auch das Arbeiten mit Schablonen.

JUST sieht sich in seinem Schaffen beeinflusst durch die Graffiti-Artists **ACDC**, **SEL** & **DANGO** und die Street-Artists **Blek le Rat**, **Breakdown** und **Mente**. Und so verwundert es nicht, dass er nun den Bogen zurück zum klassischen Graffiti spannt und als Experiment symbiotisch mit beiden Kunstformen arbeitet. **JUSTs** Idee dahinter ist das Etablieren seines Namens, quasi ein „Branding", wie es in der Werbung üblich ist. Auch wenn dies den Zielen und der Arbeitsweise der Graffiti-Szene entspricht, sind **JUSTs** Ziele doch weiter gesteckt. Aufgrund seiner Arbeit als Street-Artist ist das Forum für die Umsetzung seiner Inhalte ein anderes als üblich, so dass er damit wahrscheinlich auch differenzierter wahrgenommen wird.

JUST ist unter anderem mit **Doc Knightfield** und **Caligula** auf den Straßen unterwegs und sieht sich den Crews **RYC**, **USW-Crew** & **515 Km/h** zugehörig.

*Those who wander around Berlin looking up towards the sky will inevitably see the large letters that often adore the walls of buildings towards their tops. And, time and again, such writings are accompanied by the name **JUST**. One wonders how these enormous letters can be written on these seemingly inaccessible places. The answer is **roll-on technique**. **Roll-ons** are created using broad wide rollers and paint, which guarantees a quick and, above all, extensive application of the paint. When one works from above – from the roof – then the roller extension is simply extended and the surfaces that were inaccessible before can be reached.*

***JUST** originally comes from the Ruhr and then lived for a long time in Edinburgh, where he also studied, before moving to Berlin. He made his first attempts at creating urban art in the fifth and sixth grades when he explored **graffiti**. The Hip-Hop related graffiti culture provided **JUST** with a platform on which to express himself. Over time, however, he came to regard "name-writing" and crew-related "tagging" as too egotistical and thus found a way to create more graphic representations. Between 1999 and about 2002 he initially only made posters and stickers with anti-capitalistic, anti-sexist and anti-fascist slogans; later on he began using many other common Street Art techniques, including the employment of **stencils**.*

*With regard to his works, **JUST** sees himself as influenced by the graffiti artists **ACDC**, **SEL** & **DANGO**, as well as by street artists **Blek le Rat**, **Breakdown** and **Mente**, which is why it is not surprising that he has now gone full circle and returned to classic graffiti and works symbiotically with both art forms as an experiment.*

***JUST's** basic idea is the establishment of his name, as a kind of "branding" like that commonly used in advertising. Even though this corresponds to the goals and working methods of the graffiti scene, **JUST**'s own goals are more far reaching. On account of his working as a street artist, the platform for the transcription of his ideas is unusual leading him to be perceived of in a more differentiated manner.*

***JUST** is out and about with other street artists, including **Doc Knightfield** and **Caligula**, and feels akind to Crews **RYC**, **USW-Crew** & **515 Km/h**.*

JUST

ABOVE
JUST
JUST-ABOVE

JUST
HELLO

Lise-Meitner-Str.
45
TEPPICHLAND
BERLIN
BERLINS GROSSES
ORIENTFACHGESCHÄFT
JUST
ARAL
ultimate
SuperWash
Diesel 126⁹
Benzin 146⁹
Super 146⁹
SuperWash

CLOOZY HABER

JUST
RYC

Impressum

Originalausgabe
7., abermals aktualisierte Auflage 2016

www.jaron-verlag.de
Übersetzung: Miriamne Fields, Berlin; Marie Frohling, Berlin
Umschlaggestaltung: Kai Jakob, Berlin (abgeb. Werk: Blu mit JR @ Planet Prozess, 2007, www.artiu.de, Cuvrystraße, Kreuzberg)
Text El Bocho: Auszüge aus einem Text von Ingrid Raab, Galeristin
Text Emess: ATM Gallery, Berlin
Satz und Layout: Kai Jakob, Berlin
Alle Bilder: Kai Jakob, Berlin
Druck und Bindung: BGZ Druckzentrum GmbH, Berlin

ISBN 978-3-89773-778-5

Danksagung

Vielen Dank für die Unterstützung: Jaron Verlag, das Elternhaus, Sebastian „Brettspiel-Schummler" Steiner, speziell Boris Niehaus, Dr. Joanna Maria Olchawa, Lutz Henke, Marc Scherer, Jochen Küpper, Dr. Illaria Hoppe, Ruede Hagelstein, Sven „Fourty" Fortman, Wolfgang Reiher, Matthias Kohn, C. Stammnitz, Dörthe Gössler, alle Freunde und Förderer, Unterstützer und Kritiker sowie all die vielen netten Menschen, welche sich für mein Buch entschieden haben.
Außerdem: Dr. Norbert Jaron, Jenny Rühmer, Jana Heisel, Christiane Geißler, Dietlind Grüne, Alexandra Wenzel, Sofie Schenkel, Lisa Heinrich, Henrik Neugebauer, Dörthe Gaettens, Friederike Edner, Markus Kavka, Susanne Riethmüller und IQ Style, die nette Frau bei ARTE Kultur, Gabor, Monika und der coole Kamera-Typ von MTV Hungary, „Meine Beine sind nicht Deine" Nils Bokelberg mit Roman Libbertz von Lettra „Die Blog Show", TVBerlin, Motor FM, Willy und TraceTV, Electronic Beats Magazine, Lodown Magazine, Freestyle Magazine mit Nele und Jason, Prinz Berlin, 030 Berlin, Ozon Magazine, Tagesspiegel, Berliner Zeitung, Welt am Sonntag, dpa, Berlinpiraten, Berlinomat, AusBerlin und und und ...
Spezieller Dank: JUST, El Bocho, JR, Emess, XOOOOX, VHILS, SP 38, Circleculture Gallery, Urban Grassroots – Planet Prozess, Backjumps – The Live Issue, X-lab Kreuzberg, Urban Affairs Berlin und Urban Affairs Berlin Extended sowie Riot Arts, www.artitu.de, Urban Nation ... und all die anderen, die mich inspiriert, mir geholfen und mich unterstützt haben und die ich versehentlich vergessen haben könnte. Danke!

Danke selbstverständlich auch an alle anderen Künstler: CUPK, Karl Toon, Fuck Your Crew, Thief, Schattenkörper, Nomad, Banksy, Kowalski, Brainsen-Comix, Pank, Dolk, Die Made, Bronco, Invader, Kill your Gender, Esther Sonnenkind, Icon, Blek le Rat, Stefan M, Aem, Scharf, Sabotage, Red Ink, Selbstmordparty, Maros, Funk 25, Flower, Swoon, Gould, Evol, Skewville, Hannibal Vector, Shepard Fairey, Just, Torso, Lemming, The London Police, Above, Bild, Boxi, Faile, TGS, Faile, Akay, Bäst, Kaktus Crew, Pablo Fiasco, Alison & Solovei, Uwaga Inwazja, Bonk, Blues Brothers, Various, Okay, Robot, Miss Van, Thomas B, MCity, Blu, JR, Guy, ChinChin, Ash, Husk mit Navn, Dave the Chimp, Corto, Akim, Klub7, Pisa73, Unbewacht, Karski, Cow, Kasi, Busk, Spunk Pocahontas, Vecjuctrn, Bösa Butch, Vec, Influenza, No Logo, SMP, Doma, El Tono, Nuria, Gogoplata, Mikado, GRL, Süsswarensündikat, Grafpro, Wow, John 08, Bug, Bimer, Rui, Krazr, Ony, Eddek, Pirate Pearl, Jakob, Fase, Czarnobyl, Gomez, Arizone, Ortica Noodles, Zibe, Samc, Sam Crew, MTO, Stroke, Base 23, Tom 14, Los Piratos, Pixel Population, Booty, Toasters, TGS, Baron, 1010, Tika, Lalet, Urban Safari, Dicide, Ovni, Marek, Other, Wurstbande, Moki, Kasimir, McCoy, Dazed, Chunko, Zosen, Interbrigadas, FKDL, Faith 47, Rero, Armsrock, Neozoon, Christian Paine, Joska, Los Piratos, Castro, Ortica Noodles, Obelisk, 2501, Ema, Kain Logos, Kollektivet Livet, Roa, Kola, IR 6, Urkel, Filoart, Rubin, Sam 3, Tower, Dolk, Alias, Linda's Ex, Cream, Globalodromia, Blo, Vhils, Superblast, Santiago Sierra, James Bullough, Karl Addison, PAOD, Hannes Höhlig, JBak, Tristan Eaton, Handidan, Daleast, Rone, Dabs Myla, Don John, Shepard Fairey, Twoone, Case, JS, Jimmy C., Broken Fingaz, Icy and Sot, Alice, Jaz, Erez Israeli, Kurar, Kkade, Nevercrew, Ripo ... und alle anderen urbanen Künstler, die unsere schöne Stadt so vielseitig mitgestalten, aber hier unabsichtlich nicht aufgeführt sind oder anonym bleiben wollen.
Ohne euch wäre dieses Buch niemals möglich gewesen und die Wände unserer schönen Stadt Berlin nur halb so interessant und vielfältig, bunt und außergewöhnlich.
Danke und Respekt!

Für Updates, News etc.:
www.facebook.com/STREETARTINBERLIN

Links Street Art National: http://just.blogsport.eu; www.reclaimyourcity.net; www.riot-arts.com; www.artitu.de
Links Berlin Galleries: www.atmberlin.de; www.circleculture-gallery.de; www.openwallsgallery.com; www.urban-art.info/; www.skalitzers.com; www.urbanspree.com; www.urban-nation.net/de/
Links Street Art International: www.woostercollective.com; www.grafittiresearchlab.com; www.brooklynstreetart.com